First Published 2021

© Nick Bradfield and Jim Conboy

Text and illustrations © Nick Bradfield and Jim Conboy
Text © Nick Bradfield and Jim Conboy
Photos (NB) © Nick Bradfield
Photos (JEC) © Jim Conboy (enquiries@chartridgephotographic.co.uk).
Dates where given are processing dates (for colour slides).
Undated photographs (mostly B&W film) were
taken between 1976 and 1985.

Maps
Maps of 1956 and 1894 are reproduced with the
permission of the National Library of Scotland.
Kings Cross in 2001 - with the permission of OpenStreetMap.

All rights reserved. No part of this book may be reprinted or reproduced in any form or by any electronic, mechanical or other means, now known or hereafter invented, including photocopying and recording, or in any information storage or retrieval system, without the permission in writing from the publishers and copyright owners.

The contents of this publication are believed correct at the time of printing. Nevertheless the publisher can accept no responsibility for errors or omissions, changes in detail given or any expense or loss thereby caused.

Published and Printed by Mapseeker Digital Ltd, Unit 15, Bridgwater Court, Oldmixon Crescent, Weston Super Mare, North Somerset, BS24 9AY
Telephone +44 (0) 01922 458288 +44 (0) 7947107248

British Library Cataloguing in Publication Data
A catalogue record for this book is available from the British Library

ISBN 978-1-84491-890-4

Gasholders and Lost King's Cross

Photographs by
Nick Bradfield and Jim Conboy,
residents of Stanley Buildings

Foreword

This is about the area between King's Cross and St Pancras stations, not about the stations themselves. The scene was dominated by gasholders to the north, all now gone except for four which were put into storage and then relocated opposite St Pancras Basin. Three of these now contain housing and one a pocket park. Gasholders are as fascinating as steam engines.

Nick and Jim lived in flats in Stanley Buildings between March 1976 and August 1985. It was a unique and stimulating place to be. What had originally been Victorian railway workers' tenements were at the time owned by Camden Council, but licensed for occupation by members of SCH (Short-life Community Housing- an association originally formed by students in Camden).

During this time we were keen photographers covering many areas of London, and well aware that the King's Cross area would not be developed until central government formulated a comprehensive strategic plan - which did not happen until twenty years after these photos were taken. The buildings were unchanged from the Victorian era although there had been some changes in road layout and renaming of streets. Then very rundown, they were a great backdrop for photography and filming and were extensively used as such. Our photos are intended to capture the urban grittiness of the area particularly with the shots from the roofs of Culross and Stanley Buildings and those taken at night.

The locations photographed lie between the stations up to Goods Way, Camley Street to the north of Goods Way and the northern part of Pancras Road on the western side of St Pancras Station - now demolished and a concrete wasteland. The areas now known as Granary Square and the Coal Drops were inaccessible when we were photographing. The whole of the King's Cross redevelopment area has lost its prestigious NW1 postcode and is now designated as N1C.

Looking back forty years since these photos were taken, it is clear that the new King's Cross has little of its past to relate to. Pancras Road, Camley Street and Goods Way have all been realigned. In the area bounded by the two stations and Goods Way only two of the original Victorian buildings remain, the German Gymnasium and the Clarence Passage building.

We were fortunate to have been there at the right time to create a unique record of an urban landscape, now lost forever. We miss it every time we visit.

Gasholders and Lost King's Cross

Contents

Foreword..2

The Gasholders..4

Stanley Buildings...10

Clarence Passage..22

From the Roofs of the Buildings...........................32

Culross Buildings and Battle Bridge Road..........46

Camley Street..50

Pancras Road...62

Gasholder Gallery...68

History of Stanley Buildings..................................76

Maps..77

Photographers pictured in the '70s......................80

The Gasholders

Goods Way and Camley Street from the roof of Stanley Buildings, before the creation of the scrapyard (NB)

From the roof of Culross Buildings. The lamp post in the centre is on the corner of Goods Way and Camley Street. (JEC)

The Gasholders

St Pancras Station from Camley Street (NB)

Corner of Goods Way and Camley Street. (NB)

The Gasholders

From the roof of Culross Buildings.
The gasholders were in the process of being repainted in the original
gas company livery of black, with red and white detailing (JEC)

Goods Way, taken from the junction with Camley Street (NB)

Stanley Buildings

Stanley Buildings from the roof of Culross Buildings, looking west
towards the great arch of St Pancras station,
with the BT tower in the background.(August 1983, JEC)

Stanley Passage from the roof of Culross Buildings again looking west
(August 1983, JEC)

Stanley Buildings

Stanley Passage, looking west, towards the railway arches beneath the platforms of St Pancras - (April 1977, NB)

Stanley Passage, looking east towards Culross Buildings - (April 1977, NB)

Stanley Buildings

Decorating Stanley Passage, looking east - (September 1979, NB)

A rainy day in Stanley Passage, looking west .
The Covent Garden Supply Company warehouse obstructed the view
of the Gasholders from the lower floors of the buildings. (March 1981, NB)

Highlighting the warm rust colour of the Covent Garden Supply Company wall. Sapling planted by Camden Council– (May 1981, NB)

Stanley Buildings stairwells were steep and spiral, giving access to the balconies and the roof – (February 1980, NB)

Stanley Buildings

Clarence Passage Balconies (JEC)

Stanley Passage Balconies,
in a decorative cast iron design (JEC)

Stanley Buildings

The residents could hear platform announcements from their balconies (JEC)

Battle Bridge Road looking west towards the bridge under the St Pancras main line railway, now replaced with a much larger structure further North. The flat roof building at the junction to the right is the Gaswork engineer's residence.
(February 1981 NB)

Clarence Passage

The Clarence Passage building has been renovated and melded into a taller modern building at the back. It is now a conference venue, claiming "an incredible roof terrace, dotted with original chimney pots and brickwork, which offers incredible views and space for 40 people". However, it does not have the 360-degree views from the roofs of the old Stanley Buildings depicted in these photos. This building has confusingly been named "The Stanley Building" thus removing any reference to the original layout or location of Stanley Buildings.

Clarence Passage looking west; The German gymnasium is to the left
(September 1979, NB)

The Clarence Passage building, taken from Cheney Road, now part of "Pancras Square". (August 1983, JEC)

Clarence Passage looking east with Culross Buildings in the distance - the intervening space is now "Pancras Square".
Pancras Road now runs through the wall on the left (April 1977, NB)

Clarence Passage in the shadow of St Pancras Station looking west
(September 1979, NB)

Stanley Buildings Garden

The garden was a community project started by the residents, originating from a lorry load of spoil which a passing lorry driver was invited to dump in the middle of the courtyard. It was a green oasis for the residents, and the venue for a number of Stanley Building parties, featuring a lawn, pergola, several flower beds - and a waterfall constructed from an old bath and a bicycle dynamo. It continued to mature over the next twenty years until demolition.

After we left, a mural of two "Art Deco" dancers was painted on the entire flank wall facing Pancras Road and became a landmark.

Stanley Buildings garden from the roof (August 1982, NB)

Clarence Passage is behind the wall at the top of the picture. The realigned Pancras Road now runs through this garden and the western Stanley Passage Building, from where this photo was taken.

The garden in the shadow of St Pancras Station
(August 1982, NB)

Looking towards the St Pancras Station signal box (August 1982, NB)

Stanley Buildings Garden

Clarence Passage is behind the wall to the right and the German Gymnasium can be seen behind that (July 1981, NB)

Culross Buildings can be seen in the distance (August 1982, NB)

The rear of the Stanley Passage buildings,
from the pergola (July 1981, NB)

The punk rock band "Sore Throat" lived in Stanley Buildings.
Rehearsing for a party in the garden (July 1977, NB)

Stanley Buildings Garden

A courtyard at the rear of Stanley Buildings (May 1981, NB)

Cheyne Road from the Stanley Passage Building (March 1981, NB)

This is now the site of "Pancras Square". None of these buildings remain apart from those on the top right hand side which are part of King's Cross Station. The entrance to Stanley Buildings courtyard and garden is at the bottom of the picture.

From the Roofs of the Buildings

East side of St Pancras Station, and the (Grade 1 listed) clock tower by Gilbert Scott (July 1984, JEC)

...and in snow. (NB)

St Pancras Station - the "Barlow shed"
now obscured by a new flat roof extension. (May 1981, NB)

Fire in the roof of St Pancras Station (May 1980, NB)

From the roof of Culross Buildings, the German Gymnasium is to the left, Stanley Buildings in the Centre and the Covent Garden Supply Company in the low buildings to the right (JEC)

From Clarence Buildings roof looking
over Stanley Buildings towards the Gas Works (JEC)

Looking east towards Culross Buildings and King's Cross Station.

The V shaped structure was the 'moto-rail' loading area, and has now been redeveloped as "Pancras Square" (NB)

Footballers playing in the "Tennis Court" which was between Pancras Road and the western Stanley Passage building now demolished.
The realigned Pancras Road now runs through it (NB)

Pedestrians at the Junction of Stanley Passage
and the old Pancras Road (NB).

Gasholders and Lost King's Cross

Stanley Buildings roof looking west towards Euston Tower,
home of Capital Radio at the time (NB)

Stanley Buildings roof looking west towards the BT Tower (NB)

From the Roofs

Access to the roof in snow (NB)

Reflections of chimney pots.
The roof served as the setting for several art installations by residents. (NB)

Culross Buildings and Battle Bridge Road

Culross Hall and Buildings, in Battle Bridge Road.
The buildings and roof were used as a location for 'The Missionary',
filmed in 1982 and starring Michael Palin (JEC)

View down Battle Bridge Road towards St Pancras railway bridges (JEC)

Corner of Culross Buildings and Battle Bridge Road, in a snowstorm(NB)

...and in the rain (March 1981, NB)

Camley Street

During the time these photographs were taken Camley Street was a scrap yard on both sides. The land was bought by the GLC in 1981 to be turned into a lorry park. Local people and the London Wildlife Trust ran a successful campaign to persuade the GLC to save it from development, and create a nature reserve instead. Starting in 1983, the GLC worked with the Trust to re-landscape the reserve. "Camley Street Natural Park" was opened in 1985 and was declared a statutory Local Nature Reserve in 1986.

Camley Street (July 1981, NB)

Camley Street looking south (April 1981, NB)

Camley Street

Camley Street scrap yard looking north (April 1981, NB)
The gantry on the St Pancras main line can be seen in the background.

Camley Street scrap yard looking south (April 1981, NB)

Derelict car Goods Way (October 1981, NB)

Derelict car Pancras Road (April 1981, NB)

Detail of railway lamps in photo opposite (April 1981, NB)

Steps up to the St Pancras main line (March 1981, NB)

Camley Street north of the St Pancras main line bridge (April 1981, NB)

The "Coal Drops" building from Camley Street (March 1981, NB)

King's Cross Station is in the background, but is now obscured entirely by the redevelopment. Camley Street scrap yard is in the foreground.

Camley Street

Red Mercedes and gasholder (July 1981 , NB)

Red Mercedes and water point (July 1981, NB)

Camley Street

St Pancras main line bridge over the Regents Canal, now rebuilt.
Taken from St Pancras Basin, looking towards Camden Town (May 1981, NB)

St Pancras Basin (May 1981, NB)

This view has changed radically. The gasholders to the right have gone, replaced by the substantial redevelopment. On the left of the picture there are now four relocated gasholder frames three of which contain housing and one is a pocket park.

Pancras Road

Pancras Road was radically realigned during the renovation of St Pancras Station. The shops in the extended eastern side of the station (including Marks & Spencers and a Wetherspoons pub) are built on the line of the old road.

Demolition of one of the old railway bridges across Pancras Road at a time when St Pancras Station was very underused. (July 1981, NB)

Pancras Road - note the now illegal cigarette poster. St Pancras churchyard is on the left (March 1981, NB)

Pancras Road

Pancras Road railway arches (March 1981, NB)

The Covent Garden Supply Company -
by day and by night.

Stanley Passage is to the right of these photos (March 1981, NB)

54 Pancras Road (March 1981, NB)

Café King's Cross (NB)

Pancras Road (March 1981, NB)

Pancras Road was a notorious red-light district. Residents of Stanley Buildings were therefore quite amused at the "Cuddley Toys" sign. These buildings were all demolished to make way for the realigned Pancras Road, revealing the front of the German Gymnasium that can be seen today. Circle Thirty-Three housing association occupied the gymnasium at this time. (NB)

Gasholder Gallery

For those living in the thin triangle of land between Kings Cross and St Pancras stations, the Gasholders were a constant presence, forming the northern boundary just beyond Battle Bridge Road. While always present, they were never the same from one day to the next – sometimes a solid wall of iron, blocking the view to the north, at other times (particularly after fuelling Sunday lunch), completely flat, revealing extensive views over the canal and Camden Town behind a tracery of columns and stepladders.

During the war they were painted light grey to be inconspicuous. Later they were restored to the original livery - black gloss with red and white details on the girders – producing stunning reflections of sunsets over Somerstown.

The gasholders were originally constructed to store gas from a large gasworks at Agar Grove, just to the north. This works closed in 1904 and production was switched to the larger Beckton works. In the mid-1980s, control of the plant was automated, but before leaving the site, the supervisors arranged an impromptu tour for nearby residents, an opportunity for closer studies which can never be repeated. While their current decorative role is preferable to complete destruction, the static presentation opposite St Pancras Basin is a pale imitation of the original working structures.

Rainy day view from Flat 20 (JEC)

Awaiting removal (January 2009, JEC)

The 'triplet' structure, shortly after repainting -
(April 1982, JEC)

Gasholder Gallery

(NB)

(NB)

Gasholder Gallery

(1982, JEC)

Gasholders and Lost King's Cross

(November 1980, NB)

(1982, JEC)

Gasholder Gallery

(July 1981, NB)

Sunset behind the Hampstead Road estates
(1980, JEC)

... and from York Way bridge (1982, JEC)

History of Stanley Buildings

During the period these photographs were taken Stanley Buildings consisted of three blocks, two in Stanley Passage (originally Red Lion Passage) and one in Clarence Passage. They ran at right angles to Pancras Road which has now been relocated east and runs through the site of the western Stanley Passage building, the courtyard garden and the "tennis court".

Stanley Buildings was built in 1864-65 by the Improved Industrial Dwellings Company to provide a high standard of accommodation for King's Cross workers. It was named after their Chairman Lord Stanley. There were originally 5 blocks housing 104 families. The buildings were an early example of the use of concrete in construction - used because it was cheaper and reduced the risk of fire. The flat roofs were used for clothes drying and as children's play areas, and there was an ash chute on each balcony (each room had an open fire or a small range - hence the forest of chimney pots on the roofs). There were originally four flats per floor, later converted into two by putting a door in the entrance passageway shared by two flats.

In December 1968 Stanley Buildings was declared a clearance area by the then Minister of Housing. In May 1969 the site was purchased by Camden under a Compulsory Purchase Order and then, after improvements, the flats were leased to a housing association for five years. By January 1976 almost half of the flats were empty and were considered unsuitable for letting to families. The remaining families were rehoused in council accommodation and the empty flats licensed to Short Life Community Housing (SCH) to rehouse non-family households from other SCH properties. As each housing association tenant was rehoused the remaining flats were licensed to SCH.

In a report to the Camden Housing Development Committee on 13th May 1980 the Director of Housing reported that the flats were still considered unfit for human habitation on the grounds of repair, internal arrangement and natural lighting. The Greater London Council (GLC, abolished in 1986) already had a proposal for demolition and replacement with a coach park in two to three years' time. This was designated "Block 8" on their plans which the scurrilous residents promptly used as the title of their occasional newsletter. The residents of Stanley Buildings really enjoyed living there and formed a close-knit community participating in the running of the buildings and developing the garden.

They were keen to remain, having put a lot of effort and money into making Stanley Buildings a more pleasant place to live and with a good sense of community. They requested a minimum two-year extension in order for them to apply for a Housing Corporation grant. After consideration of the report the Housing Committee granted SCH a life of at least two years.

Stanley Buildings continued to thrive for another twenty-one years. The last SCH residents moved out in 2001 and the two Stanley Passage buildings were demolished in 2002, leaving only the Clarence Passage building - which still stands today.

Maps

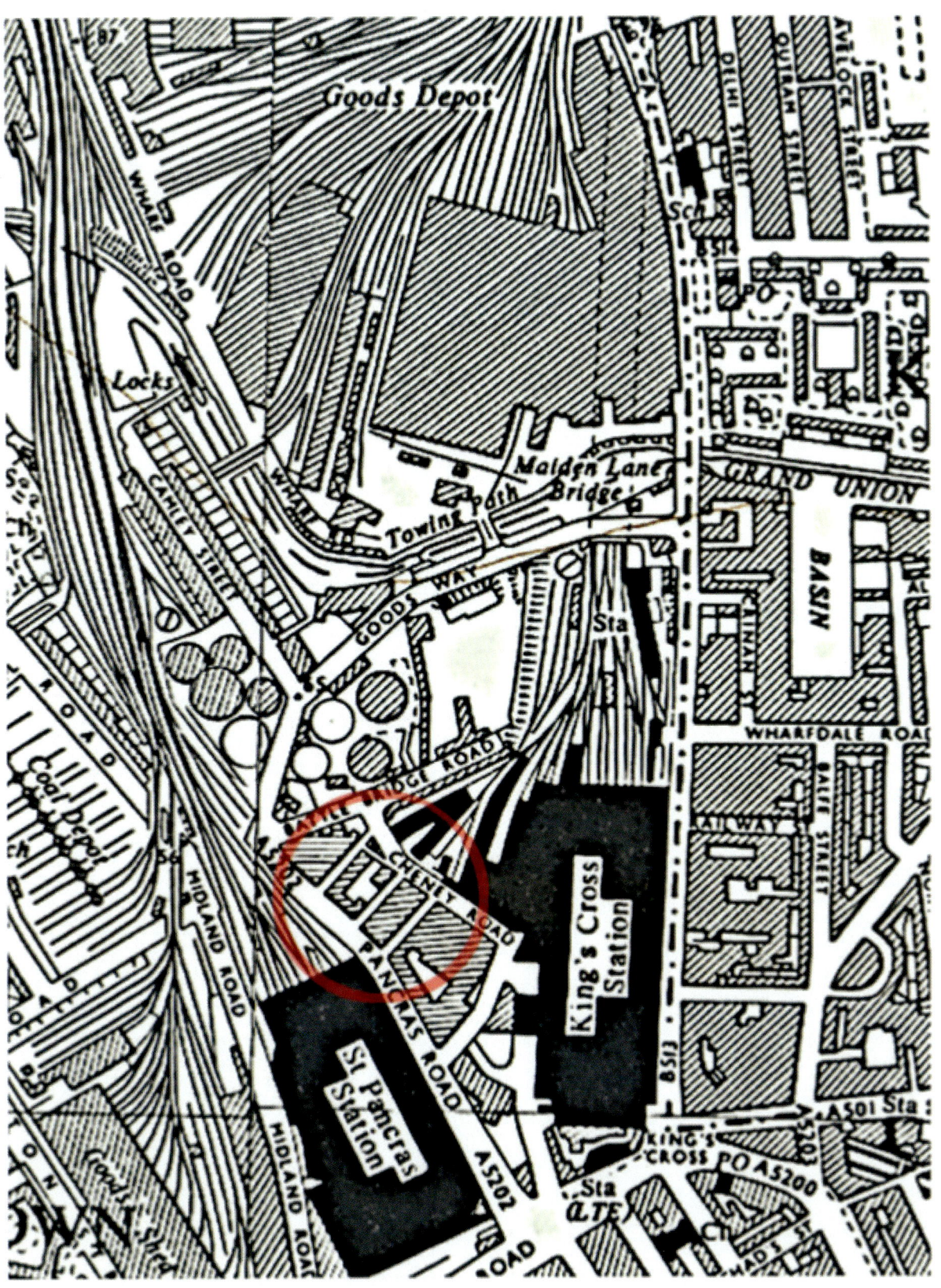

King's Cross, 1956.
Stanley Buildings and the German Gymnasium circled in red

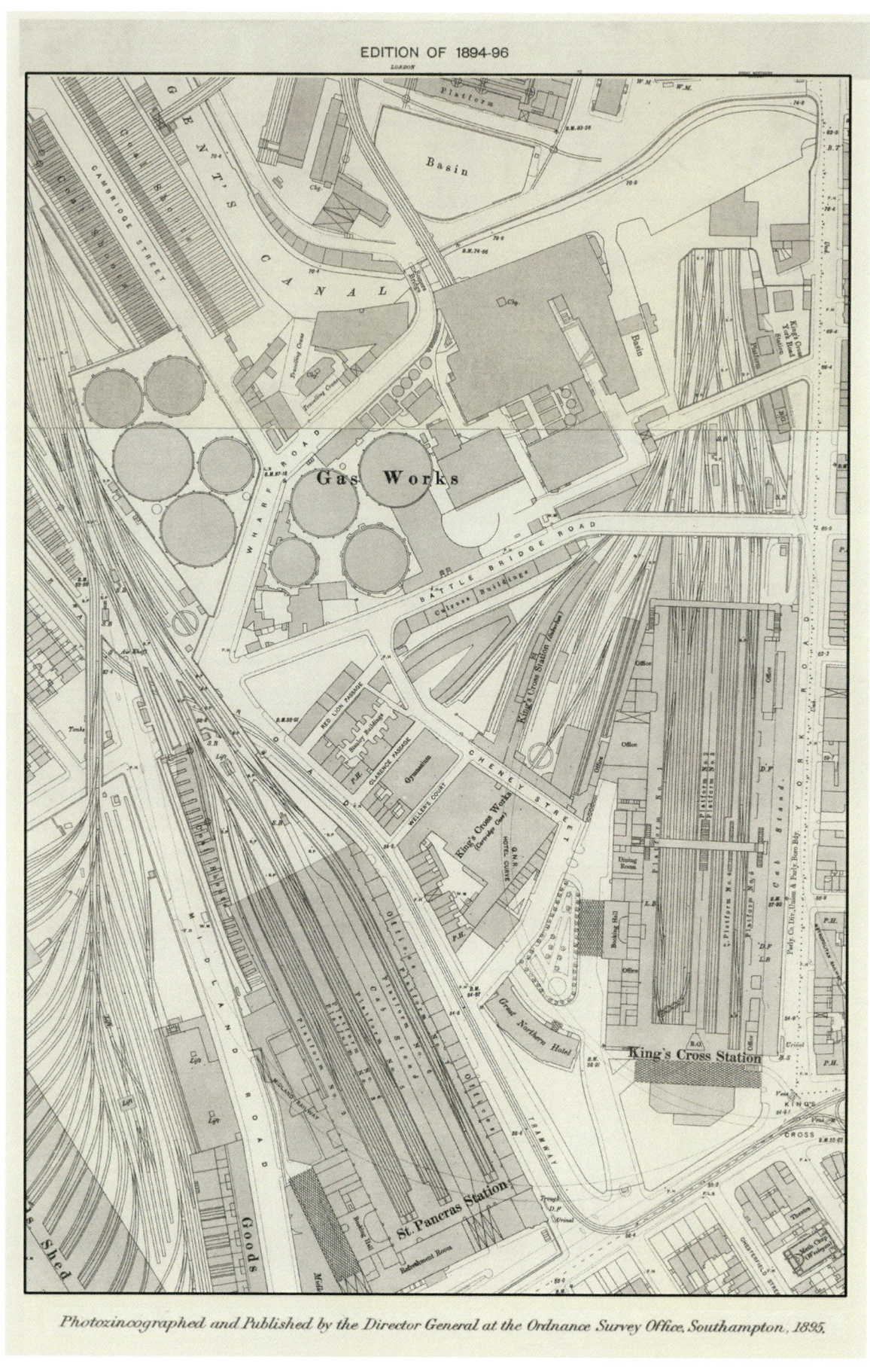

In 1894 - Gas Works and Goods Yards

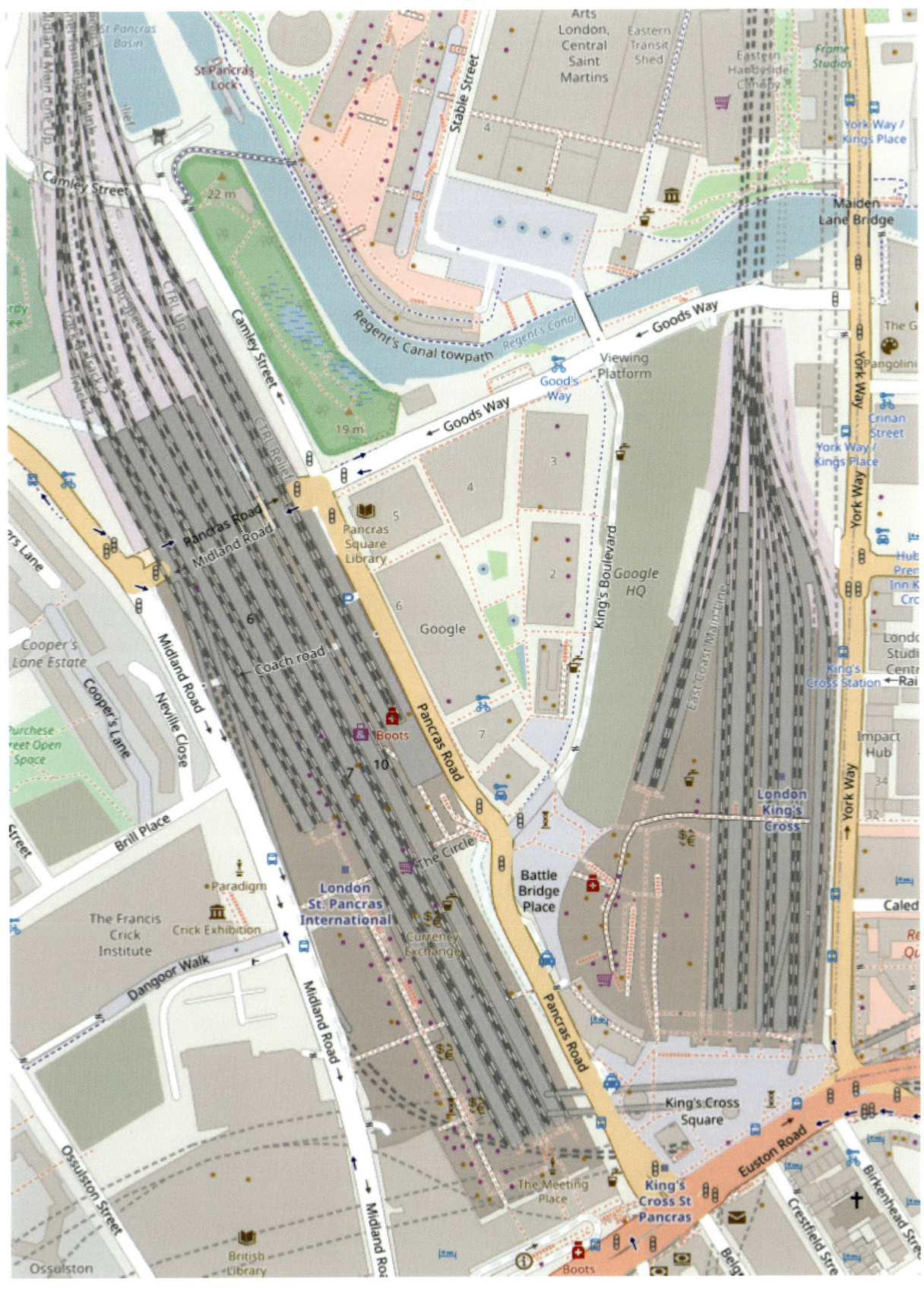

Kings Cross in 2021, following comprehensive redevelopment

Photographers pictured in the '70s

Nick Bradfield

Nick studied Urban and Regional Planning at Central London Poly during the 1970s. He went on to work in local government and then for British Standards (BSI)as a programme manager managing European and International standards technical committees . He has always taken a keen interest in photography combining it with his extensive travel both for business and pleasure. He now lives in Dartmouth Park, North London where he is involved in conservation issues.

> The pictures reproduced in this book were originally taken purely for the enjoyment of the photographers, who were fortunate enough to live in a place which provided a ready supply of striking images. It was many years later, following the complete redevelopment of the area, that Nick set about transforming our archives into a record of the King's Cross which is now lost forever.

Jim Conboy

Jim's first attempt at 'serious' photography was a response to the attempt to demolish Stanley Buildings and replace them with a coach park. He hired an Olympus OM-1 and a zoom lens over a weekend, and photographed the flats and their residents, to show Camden Council that they were no longer slums. Most of the pictures came out OK, and the buildings survived another 20 years. He later bought an OM-1 himself, and used it to take many of the pictures in this book, moving on from colour negatives to slide film. His main interests were Landscapes, particularly the Lake District, Urban Landscapes such as Kings Cross and the London Docks, and the River Thames